TORONTO

CLB 2031
This edition published by Bramley Books 1988

Printed and bound in Barcelona, Spain by Cronion, S.A.
ISBN 0 86283 638 7

The Publishers would like to acknowledge with thanks the help given to them by the Government of Canada.

TORONTO

Text by
Grace Deutsch

BRAMLEY BOOKS

Once upon a time – and not so long ago at that – a staid city slumbered by a mighty lake. Toronto the Good, as the city was known, was everything its sobriquet implied – respectable, thrifty, earnest and – dare we say it – boring.

The citizens stuffed their gum wrappers in their pockets rather than litter the streets; the politicians approved the demolition of any reminder of the past that might obstruct the progress of the present; the Maple Leafs hockey team ruled the ice at Maple Leaf Gardens; the restaurants all prided themselves on serving good "plain" food; the streets were safe to walk at night, and the whole city donned its Sunday best on the Lord's day when, eschewing the commerce it relentlessly pursued all week long, it closed down.

Today, Torontonians park their litter in the many conspicuous receptacles provided for that purpose. Feisty citizens' groups lobby successfully at City Hall to save bygone architectural gems from the wrecker's ball. As for the Maple Leafs, when they're good, they're very good, and when they're bad the groans of the faithful can be heard in every pub worthy of a draft, peanuts and a wall-to-wall TV monitor.

But hockey's not the only game in town these days. The Toronto Argonauts continue to be the local football standard-bearers – never an easy task, given the seesawing fortunes of the Canadian Football League. Soccer and basketball have fared less well: poor attendance spelled sudden death for the nascent Blizzard soccer team and basketball's Tornados.

No such fate awaits the Blue Jays, Toronto's gift to the American Baseball League and the darlings of local sports fans. Sellout crowds are guaranteed whenever the Blue Jays play ball. The opening game of the season always provokes a sudden upsurge of "one-day flu" as pinstripers, plantworkers, academics, announcers, home-makers and hordes of school kids play hookey to cheer on the Jays. Indeed, so popular are the Blue Jays that they are to be the prime occupants of a highly controversial retractable-roofed stadium, not too imaginatively called Sky Dome, which is currently under construction near Toronto's waterfront. The nightmarish traffic jams this edifice will probably cause notwithstanding, an indoor home for the Jays is in order, as snow is often a feature of season openers. Baseball and summer are synonymous in Toronto, spring being but a now-you-see-it, now-you-don't blip between the chilly winds of winter and the humid langour of the city's dog days.

Summer is also the impetus for another recent Toronto pastime – dining out, both literally and metaphorically. In fashionable Yorkville and throughout the city's many distinct neighbourhoods, sidewalk cafés and bistros overflow with the convivial chatter of the winter-weary partaking of lazy lunches or post-theatre suppers.

No matter what your tastebuds crave, you'll find a restaurant in Toronto to satisfy you. After all, there are over 4,000 to choose from! Dining out has not always been this much fun: white bread and bland were local restaurateurs' staples for more years than all but the youngest can remember.

Immigration mercifully put an end to Toronto-the-culinary-wasteland. Portuguese, Italians, Latvians, Hungarians, Japanese, Nigerians, Haitians, Salvadoreans, Ethiopians, Thais, French, Vietnamese, Russians, Chinese, Poles, East Indians, Australians, Ecuadorians, Jamaicans, Greeks, Turks, Filipinos, Ukrainians and Chileans are just some of the different immigrant groups that have settled in Toronto in recent years. All have contributed their industry and talent to the city's prosperity and their arts to its cultural life. Their culinary contribution has made Toronto one of the world's great restaurant cities.

In the new Toronto, Sunday brunch is now a regular institution, although universal Sunday shopping is still a contentious issue. Detractors of Sunday store opening cite the damaging effects of seven-day commerce on family life; supporters claim that the need for two incomes means that Sunday is the only day for families to go shopping together. Legal battles continue to rage over the issue.

Until recently, Sunday shopping was restricted by provincial legislation to recreational and cultural venues, such as bookstores and galleries, and stores in designated tourist areas. This apparently limited access was not as onerous as it sounds, because a number of Toronto neighbourhoods enjoy tourist status, and recreational and cultural outlets were – and still are – as common as pleasant eateries in most of the others. Latest developments indicate that the provincial government is going to throw the whole issue back for the individual municipalities to decide.

The notion of neighbourhoods is not unique to Toronto. New York, after all, has its Greenwich Village, its Chinatown and Little Italy, its SoHo and Gramercy Park. But, unlike New York, or other comparable North American cities, Toronto is largely free of the bruising poverty and despair that have sapped much of the joy from the urban American dream. To be sure, depressingly tasteless public housing projects such as Regent's Park and St. James Town do exist; unhappy testimonies to the urban renewal mania of the late 1950s and early 1960s. But strong citizen involvement in the running of the city combined with the advent of a farsighted Reform political movement curtailed these dehumanizing excesses before they became the norm rather than an aberration. Then, too, while Toronto aped the flight to the suburbs characteristic of post-WW II North American cities, immigration brought newcomers to fill the downtown homes of vacating would-be suburbanites, thereby saving the city core from incipient decay.

Internationally-acclaimed artist Harold Town has called neighbourhoods "the glue of cities" – and he should know because he grew up in Toronto's Swansea, a distinctive enclave of grand estates and tidy homes in the city's west end. The glue that binds Toronto together is a fascinating mix of old juxtaposed with new; of the opulence that commerce built and the tranquility and order of a day's honest labour. It's a glue of many parts, thanks in no small measure to nature herself; for the green and verdant acres of High Park have shaped the neighbourhood that has grown up around it just as surely as close proximity to the sand and waves of Lake Ontario have given the Beaches area a perennial, resort-like feel that not even the wildest winters can quite dispel.

All of Toronto's neighbourhoods are easily reached via the city's excellent public transit system. The TTC (Toronto Transit Commission), as the locals call it, is acknowledged as the safest, cleanest and most efficient system in North America. Old neighbourhoods such as Yorkville and the Annex are within walking distance of the city's commercial and cultural centre.

To understand the special character of Yorkville and the Annex, the Beaches, Chinatown, Cabbagetown, High Park, Parkdale, Rosedale, St. Clair West, Forest Hill, the Islands, Kensington, Queen Street West, Bloor West Village, St. Lawrence, Swansea and the Danforth, one needs to know something of the development of Toronto itself, for each of these neighbourhoods grew in response to conditions and circumstances that affected the city as a whole.

Long before Lieutenant-Governor John Graves Simcoe landed at Toronto Bay on July 30, 1793, to establish a secure base for the British presence in Upper Canada, the site of present-day Toronto had been a familiar landmark for the native peoples of the country surrounding the Great Lakes.

Situated on the northern shore of Lake Ontario, the wilderness lakeshore landing was the stepping-stone to an ancient Indian travel route that headed north up the valley of the Humber River, cut across to the Holland River and on to Lake Simcoe. From Lake Simcoe, other water routes finally led to Georgian Bay on Lake Huron. In those distant days of canoe travel, with its attendant gruelling land portages, the future Toronto was the meeting point of the land and water routes that crisscrossed the Great Lakes area.

The French, rather than the subsequently dominant English, were the first Europeans to explore this region. Setting out from the fur-trading base at Quebec, Etienne Brulé is believed to have travelled the *passage de Toronto* sometime in 1615. Toronto, which may have meant "Meeting Place" or "Trees in the Water" or "Lake Opening" – all equally appropriate – also figured in the Huron-Iroquois Confederacy Indian wars that raged intermittently during the seventeenth century. By mid-century, the ascendant Iroquois had established a fair-sized village, Teiaiagon, at the Humber entry on the *passage de Toronto*.

The push west from Quebec in search of new fur-bearing lands brought French fur traders, missionaries and explorers to the region, while the favourable lake harbour provided safe anchor for French supply boats. English fur traders from Albany on the Hudson also passed through Teiaiagon.

Eventually, the Indian wars became adjuncts of ongoing English-French imperial rivalry. In 1720, the French, determined to stop fur shipments from crossing Lake Ontario to the English at New York, established a post at Toronto. The post was, however, of secondary importance to France's fort at Niagara, and was closed in 1730. But the aggressive British thrust into France's

Great Lakes empire was not to be halted, and the French found it expedient to re-establish their presence at Toronto. The resulting stockade, Fort Rouille, or Fort Toronto, was built in 1751, situated about three miles (4.8 km) west of the Humber. The fort was intended to intercept the Mississauga Indians (of the Iroquois Confederacy) as they brought their furs down the Humber en route to the British in New York State.

For nine years the little garrison did its best to protect French interests. Ultimately it became a casualty of the Seven Years War: when the French lost Fort Niagara to the British in July 1759, they torched Fort Toronto to prevent it from falling into enemy hands. Two months later, the British, under General James Wolfe, defeated Montcalm's French on the Plains of Abraham and captured Quebec City, thereby ending French rule in Canada. Incidentally, the site of Fort Toronto, located in the grounds of the Canadian National Exhibition, was excavated in 1984 as part of Toronto's sesquicentennial celebrations. An explanatory plaque now marks the spot of Toronto's first military edifice.

British ownership didn't do much to alter the wilderness nature of Toronto. True, fur trading in the area enjoyed a revival – this time under British dominance. It took the American Revolution actually to start Toronto on the road to its current cosmopolitan status. It's not that fighting raged about the backwater that was Toronto – far from it. But the outcome of the revolution, in particular the peace in 1783 that reorganized the new republic and fixed an international boundary along the Great Lakes, caused the British to look more closely at the security and development of their vast northern preserve.

What was required was a strong symbol of British power to check the upstart Americans across the Lakes. Moreover, as colonists loyal to the British Crown fled north from the new republic, it became apparent that a safe centre around which the burgeoning loyalist settlements could coalesce was essential.

In 1787, Lord Dorchester, British governor-in-chief at Quebec, bought the land rights to a sizable chunk of present-day Toronto from the Mississauga Indians. The Toronto purchase was definitely a good deal for the British. For about £1,700, they acquired title to a prime 14-mile (22.5 km) stretch of lakefront real estate that ran west from today's Scarborough past the Humber to Etobicoke, with an inland depth of approximately 28 miles (45 km). Obviously 1787 was a buyer's market, unlike the present Toronto real estate scene! With Toronto real estate currently among the most expensive in North America, it's not surprising that the descendants of the Mississauga Indians are endeavouring to seek additional compensation for their former lands.

Lord Dorchester had his purchase surveyed, and a rather grand plan for the town of Toronto was drawn up. The implementation of Dorchester's vision for Toronto fell to Colonel John Graves Simcoe, the Lieutenant-Governor of the new province of Upper Canada. Upper Canada, which came into being in 1791, was intended for the predominantly English-speaking populace west of the traditionally French-speaking St. Lawrence Valley region; the latter henceforth to be known as Lower Canada.

When the Colonel arrived in Upper Canada, he established himself first in Kingston, then in Niagara, before finally settling on Toronto. Simcoe had not intended Toronto to be the provincial capital; this honour he planned to bestow on inland London. Initially he wanted a strong garrison town to keep his old foes the Americans in check. Simcoe had distinguished himself as the commander of the Loyalist Queen's Rangers during the Revolutionary War. Toronto was ideal; besides, the Toronto Passage made for a convenient open door to the riches of the Upper Lakes region.

The "national arsenal of Lake Ontario" was how Simcoe envisioned Toronto. Mrs. Simcoe, a most perceptive and highly talented woman – *Mrs. Simcoe's Diary* is still in print and provides a lively portrait of Toronto's birth – noted that the outlook of the proposed town was "indeed ... very pleasing," a fact borne out by the detailed sketches she made of the site.

Other features besides the pleasing view contributed to Toronto's ultimate ascension to first city of the province. Although Toronto's climate can sometimes be trying, with hot and excessively humid spells fraying the patience of the populace in the summer, sudden bitter blasts in winter, and spring melt-and-freeze cycles that turn sidewalks into skating rinks, the city lies outside the province's heavy snowbelt areas. Further, it was – and still is – the natural hub for the fertile agricultural lands of southern Ontario.

Taken together, all these conditions stood young Toronto in good stead, and "Little York," as Toronto was known in Simcoe's day, grew slowly but steadily. A great roadbuilder, Simcoe soon had the troops of the Queen's Rangers hard at work establishing vital trunk roads in the province. The most important of these roads, at least from Toronto's point of view, was Yonge Street (pronounced "young"). Named for Britain's Secretary of War, Sir George Yonge, Yonge Street superseded the old Toronto Passage, running north to the Holland River and Lake Simcoe, not by the Humber but closer to the more easily guarded Don River and the township itself.

Traversing early Yonge Street – actually a track rather than a street – could be a rough business: tree stumps and roots lurked everywhere to trip the unwary; rain and snowmelt made a muddy ooze of the track, and a succession of streams had to be crossed before the weary traveller covered the 30-odd miles (approximately 48 km) between the town and the end of the line on the Holland. These considerable obstacles did not, however, daunt the intrepid settlers who made their way up Yonge Street to open the lands north of Toronto.

As the province – and Toronto – grew, so too did Yonge Street. Now 1,100 miles (approximately 1,700 km) long, Yonge Street, also known as Highway 11, is acknowledged by *The Guinness Book of Records* as the world's longest thoroughfare. While the stumps are long gone, Yonge Street still has a rough patch. A short segment in downtown Toronto is the city's mini-42nd Street, complete with X-rated movies, video arcades, so-called adult bookstores and a dubious, floating, fringe population. A magnet for youthful runaways, the Yonge Street Strip, as it's known to the locals, is an ongoing subject for concern for law-abiding Torontonians.

But building Yonge Street was not Simcoe's only gesture toward assuring Toronto's pre-eminent position in Ontario, and indeed Canada. Revising his early plans for the town, Simcoe decided to move the provincial capital from Niagara to Toronto, then known as York. And although His Majesty's civil servants at Niagara were not happy at the planned move, and procrastinated for two years, Parliament finally began meeting in the new capital in 1797. In 1796, Simcoe had left Toronto for England and subsequent reappointment as commander of the forces in the West Indies. The town he laid out so carefully continued its modest growth, until the outbreak of the War of 1812.

Hostility with the Americans brought Toronto to the fore as commissary for the British forces. Not surprisingly, the astute made fortunes buying and selling supplies to civilians and soldiers alike.

Less agreeable to all concerned was the American invasion of the town on April 27, 1813. Most of York's public buildings, including the Parliament buildings, were torched. Looting was widespread. In the long run the War, with its attendant economic opportunities, benefited York. In its wake it left an expanding middle class and a small, influential moneyed contingent.

In 1834 York was officially incorporated as the City of Toronto. Although it could boast a number of handsome brick buildings – including a church for each of the major denominations – it also had its share of slums, peopled, for the most part, by the economic victims of Britain's post-Napoleonic Wars depressions.

Outbreaks of cholera ravaged the city in 1832 and 1834. The death toll was high – over 500 in 1834 out of a total population of 9,252. Fear of this devastating plague prompted the institution of daily garbage and sewage collection, and the construction of rudimentary drainage facilities.

Freedom of the press thrived, if the number of newspapers published in the town is any indication. All told, Toronto had seven newspapers: the *Advocate*, *Gazette*, *Patriot*, *Canadian Freeman*, *Christian Guardian*, *Guardian*, and the *Canadian Correspondent*. The papers represented the divergent views of the town (and the province), from the Tory-Conservative ruling clique, known as the Family Compact, through the middle-of-the-road Reformers (the object of whose reform efforts was government by the Family Compact), and the Radical movement spearheaded by firebrand journalist William Lyon Mackenzie, whose republican-sounding diatribes conjured up uneasy memories of 1812 and all that.

Mackenzie and his Radicals would probably have remained soapbox orators were it not for the world economic depression that finally overtook Toronto and the province in 1837. Farm and business failures and bank instability fed the fire of rebellion. In December

1837, Mackenzie and a blacksmith by the name of Samuel Lount led an ill-organized band of rebels down Yonge Street from Montgomery's Tavern, just above present-day Eglinton Avenue. With no particular plan of action, the rebels were soon crushed. This very limited brush with political unrest proved too disturbing even for Toronto's more liberal-minded citizens; and henceforth conservatism and the city became synonymous.

On a visit in the early 1840s, Charles Dickens remarked on "the wild and rabid Toryism of Toronto", and indeed this political sentiment enjoyed great favour not only with established Torontonians, but also with immigrants from Britain and with the sizable Protestant contingent that came over the years from Northern Ireland. The Ulster Orange Order became a considerable force in Toronto (and Ontario) politics: indeed, until quite recently the Mayor of Toronto used to dress up as Prince William of Orange and lead the Orange Day parade every July 12.

When famine in Ireland brought scores of destitute Catholic Irish to Toronto, age-old clashes between the orange and the green were inevitable. Mass Irish immigration did place great strains on the young city. Most of the newcomers were in desperate need of food, clothing and shelter, having expended all their resources to pay for their passage aboard some foul, rotten hulk.

Alas, the one thing the Irish did bring with them was typhus, which quickly spread, infecting newcomers and established residents alike. As in the earlier cholera epidemics, the city struggled to cope with the pestilence. By the time the epidemic had run its course, over 1,100 people had died, a high toll indeed, given the population of just 21,000.

The following year, 1848, brought yet another cholera outbreak, with its attendant death and suffering. Equally as catastrophic, although not in terms of life lost, was the Great Fire of April 7, 1849. Fanned by strong winds, a small stable blaze turned rapidly into a mightly conflagration that raced through some ten acres (approximately 4 hectares) of downtown property. A sudden shower saved the rest of the city, but not before a large number of warehouses and storage facilities, a sizable portion of the important St. Lawrence Market, and the venerable St. James' Cathedral, had all been destroyed.

But, as the age of the railway dawned, it was going to take more than fire or plague to hold Toronto back. For the most part, the 1850s were good to Toronto. Already the province's banking centre, Toronto was the chief purveyor of goods to and from the hinterland. To this end, its busy steamboat transportation fleet was augmented by a frenetic railway building boom. In no time, the city had rail links to New York and Montreal, Chicago and Detroit, and the Upper Lakes at Georgian Bay.

Over the succeeding years, prosperous and bustling Toronto was to spawn a new elite – merchant princes such as Timothy Eaton and Robert Simpson, and manufacturers such as the Masseys of tractor fame. Then there were railway builders and entrepreneurs, such as the Russian-born Sir Casimir Gzowski; distillery giants, such as the Gooderhams (actually, the Gooderhams were into everything from booze to banking); and the hog and cookie capitalists, such as William Davies, whose downtown bacon empire earned Toronto the nickname Hogtown, and William Christie, the original Mr. Christie of the whimsical "Mr. Christie, you make good cookies" ads.

Be the money old or new, it was housed in fine style in the mansions of Jarvis and Sherbourne Streets, Rosedale, Parkdale, and the Annex. The Jarvis-Sherbourne enclave was once one of the best addresses in town – various Masseys and Gooderhams lived here in Baronial Gothic or Victorian splendour at one time or another. Alas, the first "flight to the suburbs" – Riverdale and Parkdale in this case, circa 1890 – began the steady decline of this neighbourhood.

In the late 19th century, Parkdale was renowned for its fresh air and open vistas – in particular, its spectacular views of the sparkling waters of Lake Ontario. Parkdale was an independent and elite village until 1888, when it was annexed to the city. The building of the Queen Street streetcar line further nibbled at Parkdale's gentility, making the area all too accessible. By the 1920s, the southern section of Parkdale had become the "poor man's Riviera" thanks to the building of Sunnyside, a lively lakeside amusement complex of rides, bathing, pavilions, dance halls and boardwalk.

The Gardiner Expressway, rammed through the area in the 1950s, combined with the railway tracks, destroyed Sunnyside and seriously undermined the rest of

Parkdale. Once gracious homes were indiscriminately torn down to make way for utilitarian housing complexes that rapidly sprouted all the problems common to overcrowded, soulless accommodation.

As if all this mindless urban renewal were not sufficient, in the 1970s poor Parkdale became Toronto's unofficial "dumping ground". The lost souls mainstream society had no place for – ex-psychiatric patients, ex-cons, troubled youths, and battered women – all sooner or later found their way to Parkdale.

But there's another side to Parkdale – one that's strong and vibrant, and responsible for the gradual turnaround taking place in the old neighbourhood. Many groups of immigrants – Sikhs, Poles, West Indians, Greeks, Portugese, Filipinos, Czechs and Germans – have settled in multicultural Parkdale, bringing new energy and hope, as well as a much needed facelift, to the tired streets. At the same time, young couples eager for convenient, affordable, spacious housing in which to raise their children have also bought into Parkdale.

These newcomers with a stake in Parkdale's future have been quick to form neighbourhood associations to ensure that City Hall and the rest of Toronto give their community the fair shake it so rightly deserves. Next door to Parkdale in High Park, a tranquil domain of large, comfortable homes, tree-lined streets and, of course, the wonderful park of the same name around which the neighbourhood has developed.

High Park itself was presented to the city in 1873 by John Howard. A prominent architect, he designed the Don Jail (1836), a grimly-imposing stone edifice full of tiny, solitary cells in which the inmates were meant to while away the years pondering their crimes. Howard had acquired 165 acres (approximately 67 hectacres) of sylvan beauty on what were then the outskirts of York – the year was 1837 – with a commanding view of Lake Ontario. Here he built his home, Colborne Lodge, a charming, Regency-style structure perched on a gentle, grassy knoll.

Howard, who also taught drawing to the lads at prestigious Upper Canada College, was a keen naturalist. When he deeded his estate to the city – definitely the finest gift Toronto has ever received – he had in mind to provide his fellow citizens with a natural paradise at once educational and recreational. Howard's plan has been fully realized. Today's High Park – so named for its wonderful vistas – has grown to some 399 acres (approximately 162 hectares), thanks to additional land grants from the city. It is a shady summer retreat for picnickers, hikers, kite flyers, birdwatchers, courting couples, mothers with babies, and just about anybody who wants to get away from it all. There's a small zoo for children, rent-your-own garden plots – Howard would definitely have approved – and the Toronto Free Theatre mounts marvellous outdoor Shakespearean productions here every summer. Just bring a rug, a few cushions and a picnic supper – admission's free – but come early; lovers of Shakespeare-in-the-Park know how to stake out their favourite spot on the hills well before the stars come out.

Fall in High Park is leaf-scuffing time. It's also the best season for visiting Colborne Lodge. The Lodge, complete with Mrs. Howard's ghost – the worthy lady died in one of the upstairs rooms – was restored to its original charm after the Women's Canadian Historical Society nudged the city into turning Howard's home into a living museum in 1927. Incidentally, included among the many fascinating antiques on display at the Lodge is what is believed to be the first indoor toilet in Upper Canada. Fall at the Lodge means harvest crafts, apple-butter-making demonstrations over an open pit, the smell of freshbaked bread and hot mulled cider and cookies to warm heart and hands alike.

High Park winters mean cross-country skiing and skating, with stops for hot chocolate and roasted chestnuts. A hearty tramp through High Park and around frozen Grenadier Pond – so named for the Grenadier Guards who used to fish here a century ago – is a Boxing Day tradition for many "Christmassed-out Torontonians".

Incidentally, Colborne Lodge is not Toronto's only living museum. Other faithfully-restored treasures of Toronto's past open to the public include Mackenzie House (yes, the Mackenzie of rebellion fame), Gibson House, an elegant brick 1880s family home in the city's north end, Montgomery's Inn, circa 1830, Loyalist or late Georgian architecture at its best, and Enoch Turner Schoolhouse, the city's first free (and oldest surviving) schoolhouse.

Edifices on the grand scale include the Georgian-style

Campbell House, once home of Sir William Campbell, Chief Justice of Upper Canada from 1825-29, and the first Canadian Judge to be knighted. Campbell House was almost demolished in 1972. Public outcry and the championship of the Advocate's Society saved the building, which was moved from its original location at Frederick and Adelaide streets to the present site on Queen Street near University Avenue. Moving day was quite a spectacular event – the house, all 300 tons of it, was put on wheels and conveyed in high style to its new location.

Still queen of all it surveys is the Grange, home of the prominent Boulton family for two generations. Built around 1817, the Grange, at Dundas and Beverley Streets, is one of the oldest buildings in Toronto. Originally a country estate, the Grange was built of red brick – no wood or plastic for Mr. D'Arcy Boulton Jr., thank you – and its many bedrooms were put to use lodging famous and influential visitors to the colony. Of his visit to the Grange, Matthew Arnold wrote that he'd found "nothing so pleasant and so home-like in all our travels". Deeded to the Art Gallery of Ontario, the restored Grange now offers visitors a perfect example of a gentlemen's residence, circa 1830.

The oldest house in Toronto is Scadding Cabin. Built around 1794 by pioneer John Scadding (manager of Governor Simcoe's English estate), the little log cabin originally stood by the Lakeshore until it was moved to its present location in the Canadian National Exhibition grounds in 1879 – the year "the Ex" opened.

But if you really want to savour all the sights, sounds and smells of Upper Canada pioneer life, go no further than Black Creek Pioneer Village. Here you can chat up the "locals" about the cost of living back in the good old days, circa 1850, and watch the blacksmith, the tinsmith, the weaver and the cabinetmaker at work. There's a four-ton grist mill, using water power to grind up to one hundred barrels of flour, just as it did back when Toronto was young. At Black Creek, the militia drill, the ladies make candles and the printer cranks out the local paper down at the printing office. There are over twenty-five period buildings here, all of them bustling with mid-19th-century activity. As with all Toronto's living museums, the costumed staff not only know their jobs, be they blacksmiths, upstairs maids or cooks, they also know their facts (and recipes), which they will cheerfully share with visitors.

Sampling pioneer food is one of the chief delights of living museum-hopping in Toronto. If, however, you weary of oatmeal cookies and pumpkin pie, and yearn for the more savoury old-country cooking of Russia, Poland, Austria, the Ukraine, the Baltic States or Germany, you'll want to stay in the High Park neighbourhood or head further west along Bloor Street to Bloor West Village.

Welcome to the borscht belt. Here in deli heaven, you'll find the sweetest borscht, the softest blintzes (look under *nalesniki* on your Polish menu), the beefiest *bigos* of sauerkraut and beef, the spiciest cabbage rolls – (well maybe not *the* spiciest, the Hungarians of Bloor Street near the Annex claim theirs are spicier), plump pierogies, and pickled dills to die for.

Bloor West Village, as the Jane-Bloor area is known, is another example of citizen initiative triumphant. When the east-west subway line went through the area in 1966, siphoning shoppers off to the downtown core, the neighbourhood seemed doomed. Not so, decided the local merchants. Banding together, they raised business taxes to pay for a new look. They had Bloor Street widened, spruced up their shops and restaurants, installed benches and planted trees, which they festooned with coloured lights. To this instant ambience was added a generous dollop of East European élan: the result, Bloor Street Village, is paradise regained for all but the severest anorexic. Now the subway, which once threatened to kill the area, funnels shoppers into the Village, thereby increasing the prosperity of one of Toronto's most highly desired neighbourhoods. Lest it be thought that Polish is the *lingua franca* of the surrounding area, we must put in a word for neighbouring Swansea, whose citizens more likely trace their roots to London than Lodz.

Back in 1846, a certain Mr. Mark Coe bought 50 acres (approximately 20 hectares) of land on present day Windermere and Ellis Avenues. The area, with its quiet ponds and rolling hills, reminded Coe of Swansea, in Wales, hence its name. In time, the area was settled by the prosperous, who built solid mansions overlooking the Humber River, Swansea's western boundary. Decidedly less grandiose, but equally solid in their own way, were the homes of the white-collar workers who made up the bulk of respectable Swansea's citizenry. Both rich and not-so-rich were devoted to their gardens, a tradition that, like the very homes themselves, continues in Swansea today. Swansea only became a part of Toronto officially in 1966. Like those who marry late, Swansea's happy with the union; but don't expect her to surrender her uniqueness and independent spirit.

In direct contrast to tranquil Swansea are Yorkville and the Annex: the former, now the most glitzy – and expensive – shopping district in Toronto, the latter, colourful home to 20,000-plus Torontonians of every race, creed, age and economic status, and those indomitable champions and fearless foes of the freeway – the ARA.

No, the ARA is not an urban terrorist group, although the mere mention of the Annex Residents Association (ARA) probably still strikes terror in the hearts of a number of downtown developers and expressway enthusiasts who have had past dealings with the organization.

Neighbourhood action groups are an integral part of the Toronto scene and can claim much of the credit for keeping Toronto the eminently workable – and livable – city that it is. Perhaps the most vociferous of all these groups is the ARA. And thank goodness. For the area, one of Toronto's oldest, is rich in history and cultural diversity and is living proof that vibrant, real communities of neighbour helping neighbour can thrive – high population density and all – within walking distance of the city centre. The boundaries of Yorkville and the Annex run west from Yonge Street to Bathurst Street, and from Bloor Street north to the railway tracks, just behind Dupont Street-Davenport Road. The area is split in two by Avenue Road: you're in Yorkville if you're east of Avenue Road; the Annex once you've crossed the great divide.

Some of Toronto's most expensive real estate, both commercial and residential, is to be found in Yorkville. The Annex is not cheap either, but the neighbourhood is bohemian rather than carriage trade, and priced accordingly. Their present incarnations are something of a role reversal for the best of neighbours. Over a century ago, when the Annex was in the country, it was home to Toronto's moneyed class – as the fine old homes found here amply attest. Much of Yorkville's remaining residential architecture tells a tale of decidedly less initial affluence, present-day refurbishing notwithstanding.

The Village of Yorkville was founded by Joseph Bloor in 1830, although the official act of village incorporation didn't take place until 1853. Bloor, who was the proprietor of a brewery, had a stake in the village site, which was owned by the local sheriff, W. B. Jarvis. Conflict of interest was seldom a problem in the good old days.

Yorkville's first inhabitants worked either in Bloor's brewery or in Severn's Brewery, or else in the brickworks, then located northwest of Yonge and Davenport. The area soon filled up with neat streets of tidy – and tiny – brick rowhouses, complete with pocket-sized gardens and mansard roofs. Much of the village social life revolved around two inns, the Red Lion and the Tecumseh Wigwam, both now demolished. For those who needed to go to town to work or shop, the Toronto Street Railway ran horse-drawn cars from Yorkville Town Hall to St. Lawrence Hall every twenty minutes.

Low taxes and, dare we say it, neighbourly spirit made Yorkville a popular place to live, and not only for workers. The well-to-do moved in and built large homes on Bloor Street. On Sundays, citizens of all classes thanked God for their good fortune in beautiful St. Paul's Church (now Maurice Cody Hall), or the later Church of the Redeemer, at Bloor and Avenue Road. Incidentally, both of these churches represent valiant efforts at recreating medieval architecture, and as such are among the most interesting houses of worship extant in Toronto.

Unfortunately, Yorkville's cheap taxes – about half of what citizens of Toronto itself had to pay – were the Village's undoing as an independent political entity. In no time, the inadequate tax base translated into inadequate public services. Enter a white knight, the City of Toronto, proposing annexation and fiscal relief. Grateful Yorkville accepted, and in 1883 the Village was officially annexed to Toronto.

In time the rich departed for the Annex or Rosedale. Bloor Street itself was widened and gradually evolved into the fashionable Fifth Avenue of the North that it is today.

But to the locals, at least to those old enough to remember Paul McCartney's pre-Wings period, Yorkville was at its best when it was the long-hair and love-beads capital of Canada. Joni Mitchell, Neil Young and Gordon Lightfoot all got their start in the dimly-lit coffee houses that were everywhere in Yorkville during the mid-1960s.

The youthful hippies who patronized the Riverboat Café and its ilk, and shared earnest discussions on life, sex and Sartre, are now in their forties; the proud parents of kids who seem more interested in clothes than in giving peace a chance. Mind you, mom and dad are pretty clothes-conscious themselves these days. Come the weekend, they load their broods into the requisite BMW and descend on Yorkville from Mortgage Manor (North Toronto location a must) to buy the latest labels and designer fashions. Imports from all the great houses of Europe are readily available in Yorkville's smart stores and boutiques and are eagerly snapped up regardless of the price tags. Even Toronto babies are turned out in stylish French threads acquired in Yorkville.

As befits a high-class neighbourhood, Yorkville also offers much to tantalize the tastebuds. Specialty stores sell hand-dipped chocolates, Viennese and French pastries, fine coffees and teas, and gourmet foods from around the world.

The mind is also nourished here: art galleries abound, and showings, particularly of new and established Canadian painters and sculptors, are very well attended. Yorkville's bookstores are a serious bibliophile's delight. Foreign-language books and magazines are readily available. Readers with subject-specific tastes – for example, architecture or science – will find bookstores that cater just for them.

Yorkville comes by its cultural supremacy honestly – its near neighbours include the fabulous Royal Ontario Museum (ROM), one of the top ten museums in the world (not to be missed are the Chinese artifacts permanently housed in ROM's Bishop White Gallery), and the George R. Gardiner Museum of Ceramic Art. Situated just across the street from, and now administered by, the ROM, the Gardiner is the only specialized museum of its kind in North America. Included in this 2,000-piece collection of pottery and porcelain are priceless pre-Columbian treasures. Next door to the ROM is the McLaughlin Planetarium. For the edification of the endlessly curious, all the wonders of the universe as well as laser light shows are projected on the inside surface of the planetarium's great dome.

The Royal Conservatory of Music and the University of Toronto are just south of Yorkville, while east on Yonge Street is the Metropolitan Toronto Library. When the University's main reference library was opened some years ago, its detractors dubbed the stark, austere concrete monolith Fort Book. And indeed the Robarts Library, as it is officially called, does have an intimidating, learning-is-serious-business, feel about it. Students being students, however, the chilly architecture has not done anything to quench the flames of young love that seem to flare up everywhere in the cafeterias, corridors and stacks of Fort Book, even around exam time. The rest of U of T, whose present roster of distinguished scholars includes literary critic Northrop Frye, author Robertson Davies and Nobel chemist John Polanyi – past greats include Marshall McLuhan and Doctors Banting and Best of insulin fame – is an eclectic mix of architectural styles ranging from the Romanesque to neo-Expressionist, with everything in between.

So it took a few years for Torontonians to learn to live with Fort Book, but lest anyone think the locals are anti modern architecture on principle, we can report that it was love at first sight when the doors opened at the Metropolitan Toronto Library. Designed by Raymond Moriyama, the Library is a warm, inviting, red-brick structure that's full of plants and cosy little crannies for quiet study. There's a charming pond at the entrance, a little waterfall and glass-walled elevators which provide a panoramic view of the interior as you ascend to your subject area. The statistically inclined might like to know that the Library has capacity for 1,220,750 volumes on 28 miles (45 km) of shelves.

In addition, the Library has a number of meeting rooms for the use of the public: Torontonians are a civic-minded bunch who love joining groups and attending meetings, especially in the cold winter months. Their other great [public] winter activity is taking courses, be they educational, self-improvement or general interest. Of all the groups who meet in the library, perhaps the most interesting is the Bootmakers – Toronto's Sherlock Holmes afficionados. The Library is a natural choice for the Bootmakers – so named because young Sir Henry Baskerville in The Hound *of the Baskervilles* had a pair of black boots bearing the maker's imprint "Myers, Toronto" – because it is home to a marvellous collection of Sherlockian memorabilia and an extensive holding of Sir Arthur Conan Doyle's famous stories in different editions and many languages. The combined collection is housed in a replica of the brilliant detective's Baker Street Library, complete with Holmes' violin, pipe and slippers.

Murders most foul and other heinous crimes are often committed – at least on celluloid – in the Annex, Yorkville's sister neighbourhood. Metro Toronto is second only to Hollywood and New York City as a movie production centre, and the Annex, with its handsome old houses and tree-lined streets, is often called upon to stand in for foreign cities where prohibitive costs make on-location shoots unfeasible.

While it's possible to shoot movies in the Annex, it's a lot more difficult to drive through the area – one-way streets abound and it's almost impossible to find a parking space. It's the type of neighbourhood best seen – and experienced – on foot or bicycle, the means of transport most favoured by Annex residents themselves.

Thanks to its close proximity to the University of Toronto, the Annex has a large student population – and a wonderful assortment of cheap and cheerful, mostly ethnic, eateries for the feeding of said students. For years, goulash soup and palascin*ta* held sway in this part of town – thanks to the aborted 1956 Hungarian Uprising which drove many citizens of Budapest into permanent exile in Toronto. Since then, political unrest and/or the hopes of a better life have brought newcomers from many lands to Toronto – and the Annex. Now Korean, Indian, Italian, and Ecuadorian restaurants vie with the old-established Hungarians for the chance to satisfy those hearty student appetites.

It would be wrong to think the Annex is just a student enclave. It's not. It's home to families with kids (finding a day-care space is almost as hard as tracking down a parking spot), elderly widows who wouldn't dream of leaving their rambling old houses for a nursing home (although the area does have its share of these facilities) and communes, both artistic and economic – Toronto has an almost zero apartment vacancy rate, so finding an affordable place to live calls for great ingenuity and a willingness to share. The old mansions of the Annex shelter battered wives and troubled teens, provide opulent settings for the exclusive clubs of Toronto's elite, and offer space for public-spirited institutions as diverse as the Italian Cultural Institute, Outward Bound, and Pollution Probe's model home, Ecology House. Renovated attics and basements are choice work spaces for writers, artists, editors, musicians and "Bay Street holdouts", those idealistic lawyers who prefer human rights and immigration law to high-paying corporate work in the business district.

Annex ambience owes much to the area's architecture; fanciful Queen Annes with their turrets and gables abut sturdy Romanesque rock fortresses. Intricately carved lions and leering gargoyles adorn many houses – to the delight of local school kids. "Architecture of the Annex" is a favourite field trip for the Grade Sixes at local Huron Street School. The old school annex building dates back to 1890 and is complete with maple-panelled classrooms. And, at night, the soft light of interior lamps illuminates the ornate, multi-coloured windows that are a feature of so many area homes.

The architectural homogeneity of the Annex – the original planners passed bylaws forbidding the construction of modest dwellings and row houses – is certainly not duplicated in Cabbagetown, in the city's east end, or Chinatown, to the south of the Annex.

For years, Cabbagetown was synonymous with the working class Anglo-Irish who lived there – the name comes from the cabbages which the locals grew in their front yards. The neighbourhood was poor, but it was honest. Harder times came in the 1960s, when developers razed blocks of homes to make way for some extraordinarily unsightly apartment towers. Fortunately, gentrification came to the rescue of Cabbagetown before too much damage was done. Sandblasters, renovators and landscapers went to work, and presto, a century's grime – and the cabbages – disappeared.

But the white-paint brigade notwithstanding, the old neighbourly spirit of Cabbagetown still prevails. And while the size of their bank balances may not all be the same, Cabbagetown residents are united in their fervor to keep their neighbourhood respectable. Which means keeping the ladies of the night and their clients from moving further east from nearby Carlton and Jarvis streets. In a recent court hearing, the presiding judge sentenced a number of "Johns" to community service cleaning up the streets of the evidence of their activities – a move loudly applauded by area residents and their neighbours in Cabbagetown.

A problem perhaps more prosaic than prostitution awaits visitors to Chinatown – choosing an eating spot from the hundreds that beckon locals and tourists alike. Toronto's large Chinese community – the city's Chinatown and that of San Francisco are rivals for "the second-largest-Chinatown-in-North America" prize (New York comes first) – owes its start to Sam Ching, who opened a laundry at 9 Adelaide Street West in 1878.

Despite restrictive immigration laws and occasional bursts of ugly racism, Mr. Ching and the other Chinese who opened businesses in the area persevered and prospered. Now, a little over a century later, Chinatown is a mix of traditional greengrocers and herbalists and western-style malls with a distinctly Chinese cast.

Much of the bustling prosperity of Chinatown can be attributed to relatively recent cash infusions from Hong Kong investors, who are anxious to consolidate their finances before Hong Kong reverts back to the Chinese Mainland in 1997.

Actually, there are really three Chinatowns in Toronto: Chinatown 1, the old area where Sam Ching got started, which now runs from west of Spadina Avenue (once the hub of Toronto's Jewish quarter and still the main thoroughfare of the city's fashion district) to Bay Street, and from College Street to south of Dundas; Chinatown 2 at Gerrard and Broadview; and the growing community of Sheppard and Midland Avenues in suburban Scarborough, Chinatown 3.

But Chinatown 1 is where the action – and the best food – is, especially on Sunday, when Chinese from all over the city come to shop, dine and socialize. A Sunday feast of mussels with peppery, black bean sauce or hot pots of chicken and melon (a delectable Hong Kong-style import) should get you in the mood for a short stroll through Chinatown to see what's up at the Art Gallery of Ontario at Dundas and McCaul Streets. The AGO houses over 10,000 works of art including canvases by Rembrandt, Picasso, Hals, Renoir and Chardin. The AGO's Canadian collection includes works by the Group of Seven, Cornelius Kreighoff and Emily Carr, and Paul Peel's wonderfully evocative study of childhood innocence and joy, "After the Bath". The AGO also has the largest public collection of works by the acclaimed British sculptor Henry Moore. The Henry Moore Sculpture Centre, which was specially designed under Moore's supervision, houses over 600 of the artist's works, most of them donated by Moore himself.

When you're on Dundas Street, you're not far from two of Toronto's favourite shopping haunts: the Kensington Market and the Eaton Centre. Aside from the fact that money changes hands at both locations and both market and mall are great spots for just hanging out, Kensington Market and the Eaton Centre have very little in common.

Let us begin by saying Kensington is not for the squeamish or for those offended by the strong odours of food in its unsanitized, natural state. Here you'll find fish stalls and mounds of cheese, fruit and vegetables of all kinds – West Indian produce a specialty – freshly-killed poultry and crates of live rabbits and chickens and pigeons awaiting purchase, slaughter and consumption. Well, you were warned!

Kensington started out as the Jewish market and served the city's Jewish population before that community's migration to Forest Hill and "God's Country", as the suburban wilderness north of Steeles is affectionately referred to by Jews who continue to find the promised land downtown. Reminders of the good old days in Kensington include the Kiever Synagogue, built in 1925, and the Minsker Synagogue, which dates from 1930. While there are still some traditional Jewish stores in the market – Lottman's h*allah* is claimed by many to be the best in town (personally, we think the nearby Harbord Bakery's is superior) – most of the kosher butchers of the past have given way to Portuguese fishmongers and West Indian greengrocers. More recent immigrants such as the Vietnamese have also opened shops and stalls in the market.

Less colourful than Kensington Market, but equally noisy (unfortunately no *Fado* music, just mindless Muzak) is the Eaton Centre. Named for Timothy Eaton, the founder of the Eaton department store dynasty – "goods satisfactory or money refunded" – the Eaton Centre offers shoppers 300 indoor stores, restaurants and services on four levels. This whole complex, which also includes twenty-one movie theatres, is protected from the elements by a towering glass archway that is strangely reminiscent of Moscow's huge GUM department store. Dour Methodist that he was, old Timothy would have burned his famous Eaton's Catalogues, every last one of them, rather than admit to such a comparison. A covered walkway links the Eaton Centre – and Eaton's, its flagship store – to Simpson's, Eaton's traditional rival. It's not a particularly acrimonious rivalry, hence the walkway. From their earliest days, both Eaton's and Simpson's have benefited from their proximity, as customers traditionally confined their shopping to just these two stores.

The Eaton Centre – and Simpson's – are part of Toronto's Underground City. The world's largest subterranean complex, the Underground City starts with the elegant Atrium shopping/office complex on Bay Street and progresses south for six blocks to Union Station. In addition to the Eaton Centre and Simpson's, the City includes the stylish shops to be found in the Sheraton Centre, First Canadian Place, Toronto-Dominion Centre and the Royal York Hotel. Atop the Underground City is much of Toronto's multi-billion-dollar financial district. Incidentally, the Underground City is not without its detractors, who fear that the complex will rob the streets above ground of the people needed to keep them alive and pulsing. Supporters counter by stating that it's hard to feel truly alive wading through salty slush in the aftermath of a January snowstorm. No doubt both sides have a point.

In many ways, trying to effect a compromise in contentious issues is what Toronto is all about. It's not always easy. And no wonder. Metropolitan Toronto, the largest urban centre in Canada, has over 3.5 million people. Five cities go to make up Metropolitan Toronto – Toronto, North York, York, Etobicoke and Scarborough, and one borough, East York. Each has its own local government and representation on Metro Council. Toronto's ever-expanding populace is drawn from more than seventy ethnic groups – most of whom participate in Caravan, an annual multi-national extravaganza of delicious foods and colourful entertainment savoured by all Torontonians right in their own back yard. And there are over one hundred languages spoken here.

While this linguistic diversity contributes much to the cosmopolitan verve of Toronto, it's also the stuff rancorous political battles are made of. Should children whose mother tongue is not English or French, Canada's official languages, be taught their own first language during regular school hours or in special after-school classes? Like Sunday shopping, heritage language lessons are an ongoing subject for debate. And debate is the key word here. Although feelings run hot on such topics, there seems to be tacit agreement among Torontonians that these issues can – and should – be resolved without serious disruption of the peaceful fabric of life enjoyed by the citizenry.

Other Canadians decry this attitude of Torontonians, citing it as a manifestation of selfish smugness – the type of smugness only possible in a city that has cornered the nation's wealth and all the possibilities for the good life that go with prosperity.

Not so, claim Torontonians. They assert their city works because its citizens believe that everything Toronto has to offer should be readily available to all. And it is. The list of intangible pleasures is endless: taking the ferry to the Islands for a summer picnic, watching the kids get a charge (literally) out of their hands-on contact with science at the Science Centre, peering at the animals peering at you at the world-renowned Metro Zoo, delighting in the artistry of Karen Kain and the National Ballet of Canada at the O'Keefe Centre or the Toronto Symphony at Roy Thompson Hall, skating and sipping hot chocolate at Nathan Phillips Square in front of City Hall, partying the night away at Caribana (the giant West Indian festival of reggae, costumes and dancing), watching movies non-stop at the ten-day-long film Festival of Festivals, or chatting up affable Holsteins at the Royal Agricultural Winter Fair.

But, above all, Torontonians are united by a desire for tranquil community life. Many years ago, an admirer of the Annex commented that the neighbourhood's design bespoke the "confidence (the citizens) put in the civility and goodwill of neighbours." This civility and goodwill continue to thrive in Toronto, making the city by the lake one of the most agreeable and civilized in North America.

Oh, yes, and the streets are still safe to walk at night.

Facing page: Toronto's harbourfront.

duMAURIER
Misseli

THE WESTIN

Previous pages: downtown Toronto. Facing page: City Hall, the symbol of Toronto since its completion in 1965, and (top) University Avenue. The Canadian National, or CN, Tower (above) in downtown Toronto contains a transmission mast for radio and television. Overleaf: the Ontario Hydro building, seen from Queen's Park, in which energy given off by lighting, equipment and, indeed, people is stored underground in thermal reservoirs and recirculated.

Nati

ust
National

Previous pages: St. James Park by St. James Cathedral. Above: the Parliament buildings of Ontario in Queen's Park. Princes' Gate (top), so called because it was opened in 1927 by Prince Edward and Prince George, leads to the famous Canadian National Exhibition, or the CNE. Facing page: University Avenue lit with Christmas lights, and (overleaf) the clock tower of Old City Hall seen from the gardens of Osgoode Hall, York University's law school and home to the Law Society of Upper Canada. The iron fence put up around it shortly after its completion in 1828 was to keep cows and horses off the lawn.

Kings College (above), and Falconer Hall (top), the faculty of law offices, are both part of the University of Toronto. A farm house (facing page) and five other original farm buildings, built in the eighteenth century by Daniel Strong, a Pennsylvanian-German pioneer, form the basis of Black Creek Pioneer Village. Twenty-five other buildings were moved to the site to recreate a mid-nineteenth-century Ontario community. Overleaf: Exhibition Park, Ontario Place and Toronto's waterfront under snow.

BULOVA

Facing page: the diverse lines of Nathan Phillips Square and the Old City Hall traced by Christmas lights. Top: the painted Flat-Iron Building in the St. Lawrence Market area of Toronto, and (above) the vivid colours of Toronto's harbourfront with its waterside vendors. The most eye-catching silhouette against the sun-gilded Toronto Inner Harbour skyline (overleaf) is the elegant CN Tower.

Ontario Place leisure complex (overleaf), lit and underlit by fireworks above and their reflections below (facing page), is said to resemble "a futuristic offshore drilling rig". It was built on man-made islands bridged by walkways, among lagoons on Lake Ontario, to house technological and other exhibitions, bars and its distinctively globular cinesphere. Above: winter skating on Nathan Phillips Square's ice-bound pond.

Previous pages: suburban Toronto, the city skyline visible in the distance. The Metropolitan Toronto Zoo (these pages), set in the Rouge River Valley, places great emphasis on exhibiting and interpreting nature as a whole by recreating natural habitats from all over the world in order for a wide variety of animals to be seen as free as possible. Overleaf: Toronto's waterfront and Ontario Place fanned out in front of the slender CN Tower.

BULOVA

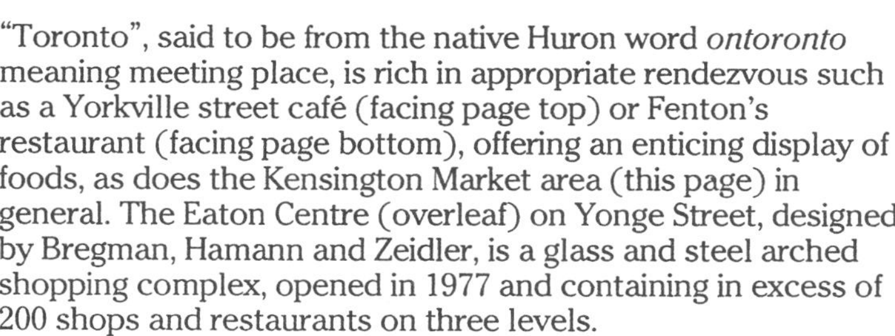
"Toronto", said to be from the native Huron word *ontoronto* meaning meeting place, is rich in appropriate rendezvous such as a Yorkville street café (facing page top) or Fenton's restaurant (facing page bottom), offering an enticing display of foods, as does the Kensington Market area (this page) in general. The Eaton Centre (overleaf) on Yonge Street, designed by Bregman, Hamann and Zeidler, is a glass and steel arched shopping complex, opened in 1977 and containing in excess of 200 shops and restaurants on three levels.

40%

CITY
Celebration
GOURMET PASSAGE
Telephones
Lockers
EXIT
EVERY SUIT ON SALE
PEGABO
EXIT

The CN Tower (facing page), just over 1,815 feet tall, dominates the skyline of Toronto with its graceful proportions, and is reflected in the glass of less tapering buildings (above) around it. Overleaf: the police pipe band in Nathan Phillips Square.

NEW SEAWAY FISH MARKET
368-1552
The Finest of The Deep! Seafoods

CHEESE
FROM AROUND THE WORLD

DANISH SHARP
Havarti
SPECIAL 1.49 lb.
OLD-WHITE
CHEDDAR
SUPER SPECIAL 1.49 lb.
YOU'LL DO BETTER AT GLOBAL
CHESHIRE LANCASHIRE 1.89
BRIE 1.89
TILSIT 1.89
CHEDDAR 1.49
PROVOLONE 1.89
OKA 2.89
MOZARELA 1.89
HAVARTI 1.89
FYNBO 1.89
MYNSTER
HAVARTI
TYBO

AUGUSTA AV
234
NASSAU ST.
DO NOT ENTER
30 MINUTES PARKING ANY TIME
Fancy

KWONGCHOW
Tavern
KWONGCHOW

Up to the Second World War, Toronto was eighty percent Anglo-Saxon, but after the war immigrants from all over the world arrived, making modern Toronto a vivid, colourful illustration of Canada's ethnic mosaic. The Kensington Market area (facing page: top and bottom left, and this page top) is mainly Portuguese, and Chinatown (remaining pictures) speaks for itself. Overleaf: the Eaton Centre decorated for Christmas.

eace
Be
To
All.
Great Indoors
Peace
Be
To
All.
FLORSHEIM

Peace Be To All.
Peace Be To All.
Peace Be To All.
City Pizzazz Cafe
Hosiery

Above: the Royal York Hotel seen from York Quay in Toronto Harbour. St. James Anglican Cathedral's ninety-seven-metre-high spire (facing page top) is the tallest in Canada. Facing page bottom: Toronto's skyline seen from Ontario Place. Molson Ontario Breweries Ltd sponsor a number of sporting events (overleaf) around Toronto. Following pages: the Blue Mountain ski resort near Collingwood, north of Toronto.

MOLSON INDY
Nashua
Coolers & Computer Supplies
Marlboro
TOSHIBA
SONY

SONY
BREWERS OF EXPORT
MOLSON EXPORT
SONY
MOTOMASTER Motor Oils
KRACO
LONGINES

BLUE MOUNTAIN
IMPORTANT NOTICE TO TSC & CSC MEMBERS. MEMBER TICKETS INVALID WITHOUT CLUB BADGES VISIBLY DISPLAYED
REMOVE POLE STRAPS FROM WRISTS
ALL SKIERS MUST WEAR SAFETY RETENTION DEVICES

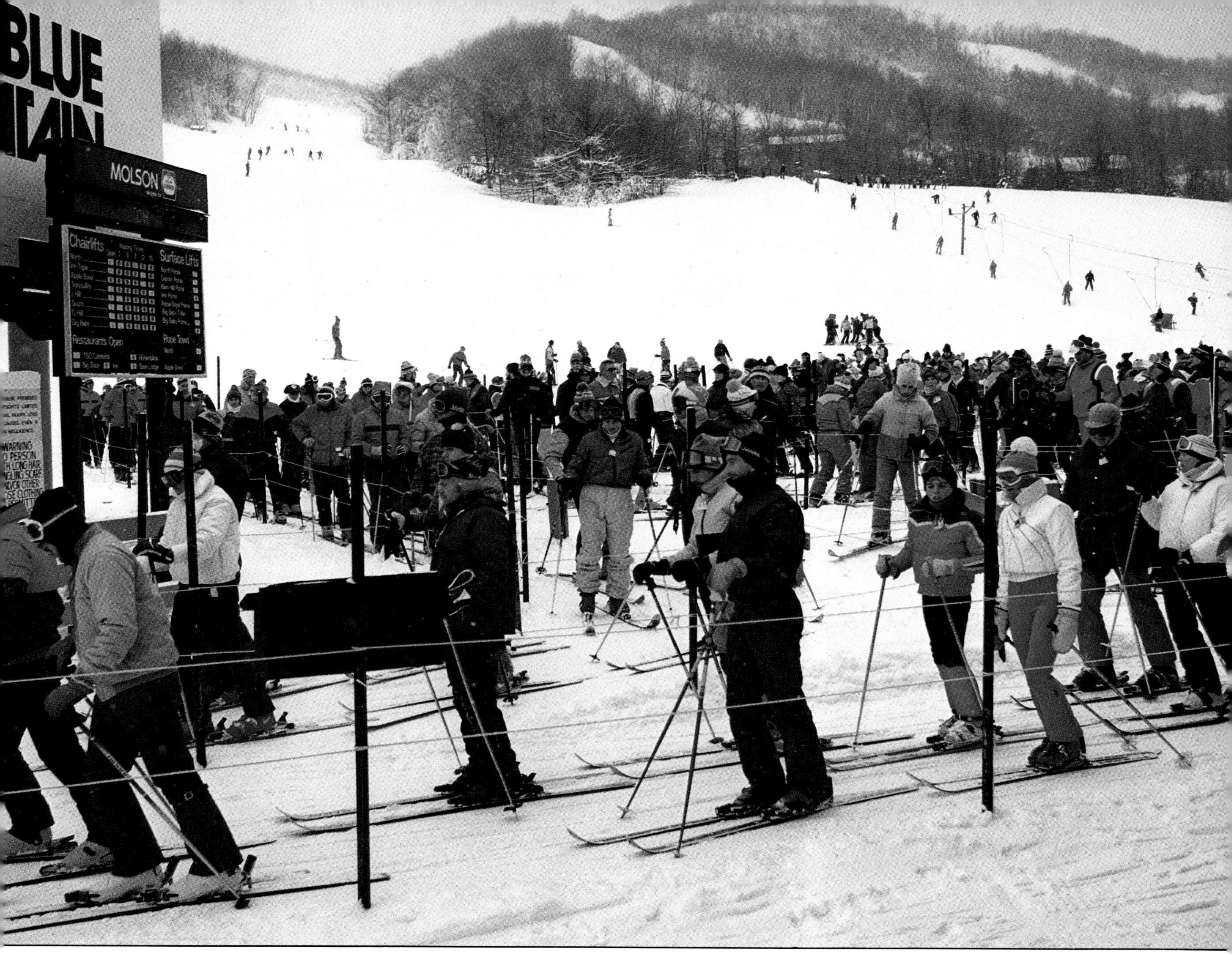
BLUE
MOLSON
Chairlifts
Surface Lifts
Restaurants Open
Rope Tows
WARNING

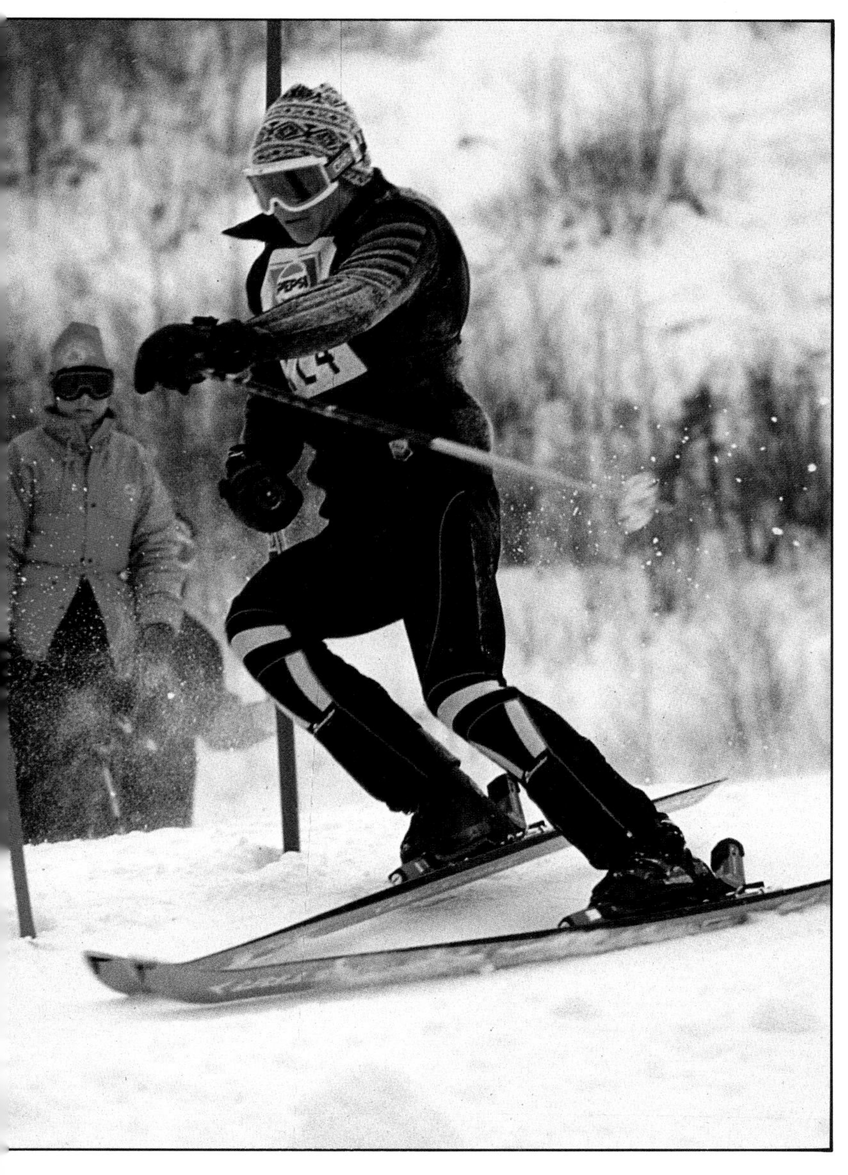

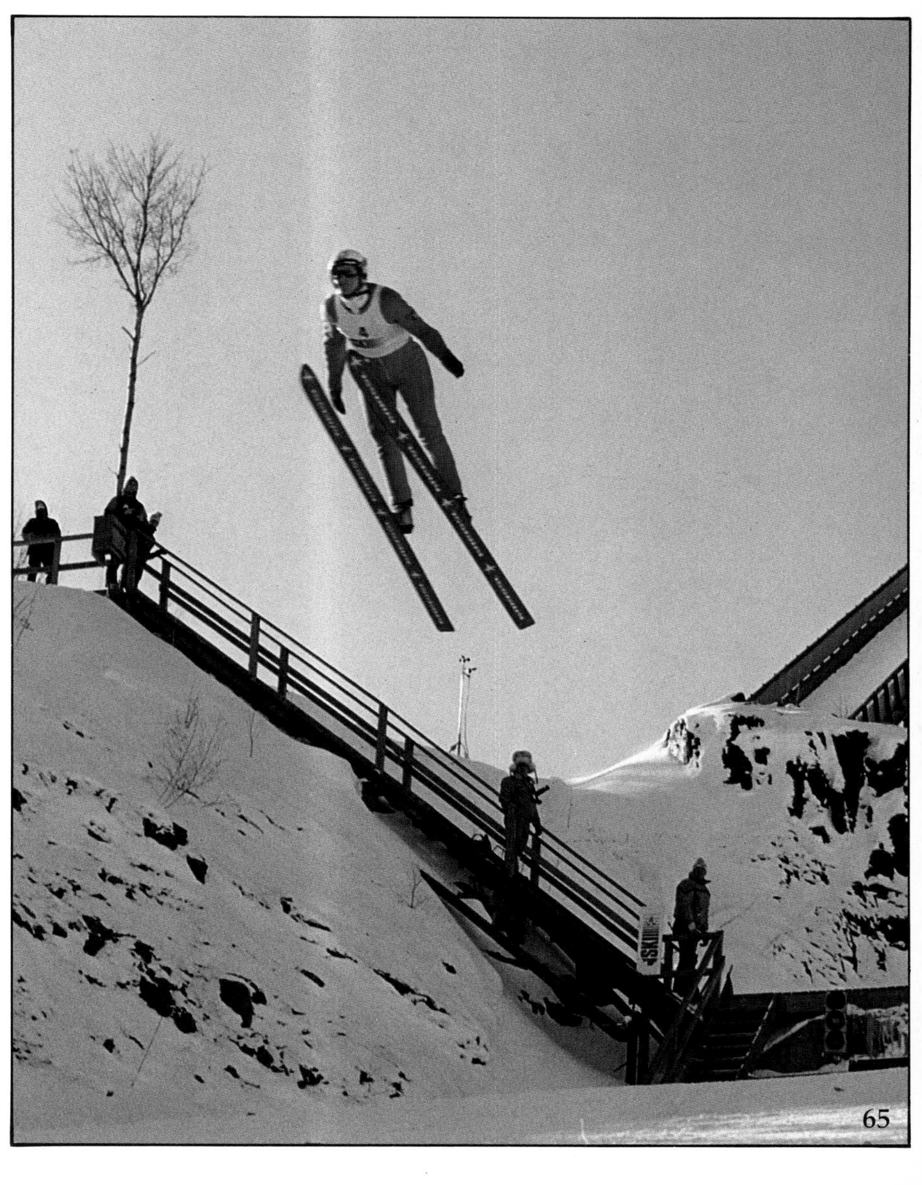

PANASONIC

Previous pages: an aerial view of Toronto's waterfront, Exhibition Park, Ontario Place and the outlying Toronto Islands making up its almost land-locked harbour. The Roy Thomson Hall (top), a glass-sheathed concert hall, is acoustically as well as architecturally striking. Above and facing page: the unmistakable CN Tower, seen from Front Street behind the A. E. LePage building. Overleaf: Nathan Phillips Square lit for Christmas.

Becker's

Edward's Gardens (previous pages) lie off Leslie Street in the Don Mills area of Toronto, lending brilliant colours to the city. Facing page: University Avenue, leading to the Legislative Buildings of Ontario in Queen's Park, which were opened by Edward, Prince of Wales, later King Edward VII, in 1860. Above: a leafy, outdoor café in downtown Toronto. The season's highlight is the running of the Queen's Plate (overleaf), North America's oldest stakes race, at the Woodbine track.

6
CHANCE FO
3
ONE FROM
STERO

Above: the skyline of Toronto mirrored in the placid water of Lake Ontario (top). St. Lawrence Town Hall (facing page), once a centre of social, political and cultural activity, was built during the 1850s and restored in 1967 by the City of Toronto as part of their centennial project to revive its former urban elegance. Overleaf: University Avenue and the Ontario Hydro seen from Queen's Park.

ST LAWRENCE HALL

Facing page: Yorkville (top left) and Hazleton (top right) avenues offer many picturesque shops and shady, open-air cafés for footsore downtown shoppers, whilst Nathan Phillips Square (bottom left and bottom right) hosts the police pipe band and a less regulated medley of street artists working under the shade of the square's trees. Above: the gardens of Toronto Islands, and (overleaf) Toronto by night, lit by a thousand office windows.

These pages: Nathan Phillips Square, containing a mêlée of street vendors, artists and passers-by. Overleaf: Christmas illuminations in Nathan Phillips Square add to the decorative effect of office lights in Toronto's dusk.

Inglis
PANASONIC
BULOVA

Exhibition Park (facing page), containing the Exhibition Stadium, where Toronto's Blue Jays play baseball, can look uncharacteristically tranquil in winter. Top: the Toronto Islands ferry tour, and (above) a yacht marina off the harbourfront.

Overleaf: walkways connecting the islands and buildings of Ontario Place in front of the cinesphere, a golf-ball-like building covered with lights, which contains a curved screen six storeys high on which films are shown.

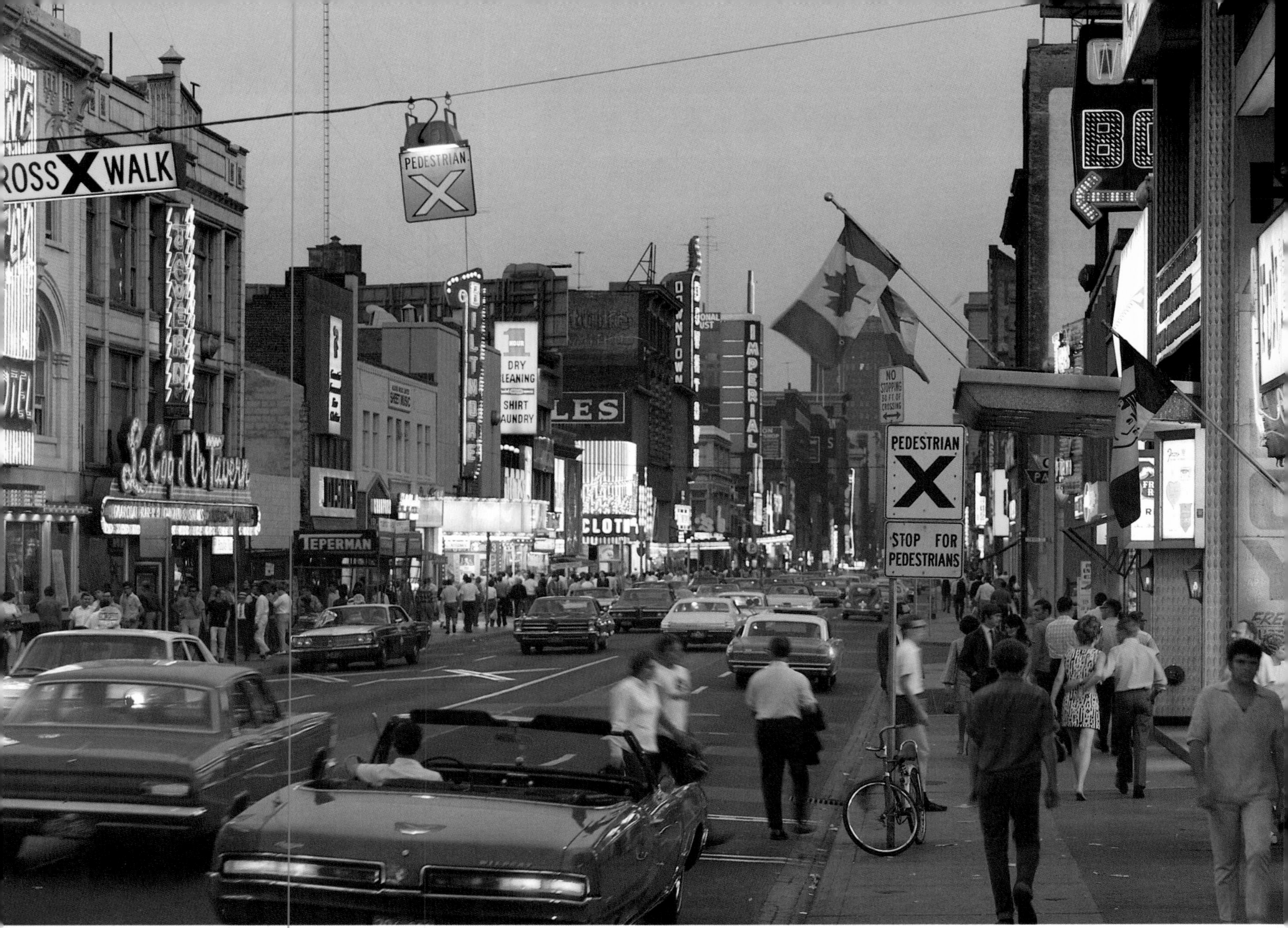
ROSS X WALK
PEDESTRIAN X
DRY CLEANING
SHIRT
TEPERMAN
IMPERIAL
NO STOPPING
PEDESTRIAN X
STOP FOR PEDESTRIANS

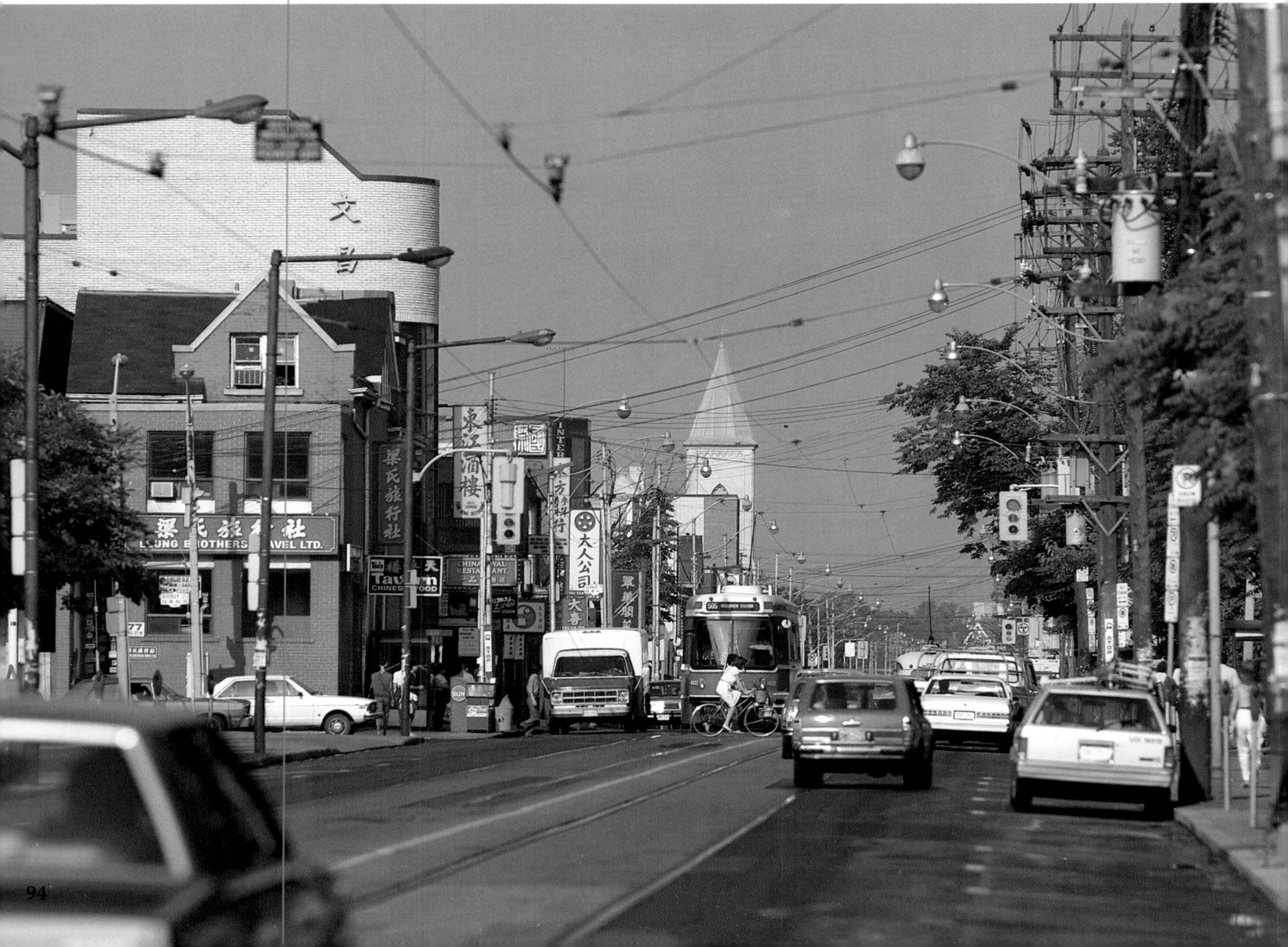
梁氏旅行社
LEUNG BROTHERS TRAVEL LTD.
大人公司

These pages: everyday activity in the streets of Toronto and Toronto's Chinatown (facing page bottom and this page top). Overleaf: the shafting light of evening crosshatches with shadows the vertical lines of Toronto's skyline.

EATONS
COLES COLES COLES COLES

St. James Anglican Cathedral (facing page) was built on King Street in 1853. Its ninety-seven-metre-high steeple serves as one of Toronto's best known landmarks, though its stained-glass (above) is equally remarkable. Overleaf: University Avenue, leading to Queen's Park and the Legislative Buildings, lit with traffic and Christmas lights.

THE WESTIN

These pages: offshore views of Toronto. Above: Ontario Place seen from the yacht marina. Facing page: (top) the ferry from Toronto Islands, and (bottom) one of the gardens of Toronto Islands. Pier 4 (overleaf), famous for its sailing schools and nautical supply stores, lies along the Harbourfront in a series of shops, restaurants and accommodation.

PIER 4
STOREHOUSE
RESTAURANT
BOGEY'S
Casablanca
CANADA DRY

ROYAL YORK
INVITATION

The University of Toronto (this page) was founded in 1827 as King's College. University College (top) is probably its best known building, overlooking Trinity College and its chapel (above). The medical school is especially famous as the department in which Dr. Charles Best and Dr. Frederick Banting isolated the hormone insulin in 1921. Facing page: (top) High Park Gardens, and (bottom) Queen's Park. Overleaf: fireworks over Ontario Place.

The Church of the Holy Trinity, built in 1847, and its accompanying building (facing page) are to be found almost secreted in Trinity Square, where they set up a solid, ivy-covered contrast to the tall glass of the Eaton Centre, designed around them. A statue of Sir John Sandfield MacDonald (above), Ontario's first Prime Minister, stands at the head of Queen's Park facing University Avenue. Overleaf: the fair at Midway in the Canadian National Exhibition.

LONG DOG ON A STICK
Ice Cream
Original SUPER DOG Factory
COLD DRINKS LEMONADE
HOMEMADE

96
18

CABINET MAKER

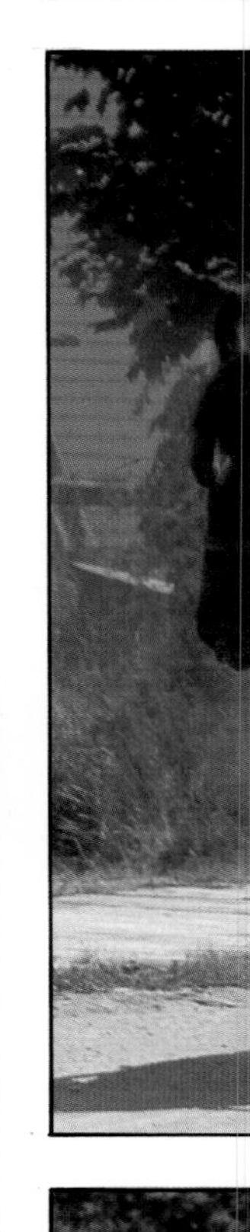

Black Creek Pioneer Village (these pages) centres on Daniel Strong's early-nineteenth-century farm. Together with the twenty-five other contemporary buildings transported to the site they preserve a sense of timeless rural tranquility despite the freeways and the closeness of York University, from which many of the costumed staff are recruited during holidays. Overleaf: the Ontario Parliament building in Queen's Park.

Just messing about in the water attracts visitors to the Toronto Islands (top, above, and facing page top). Old Fort York (facing page bottom), originally built by Governor John Graves Simcoe in 1793 to defend Canadians and British soldiers against the Americans, fell in 1813 with the American capture of the town. It was renovated in 1934 for Toronto's centennial celebrations. Overleaf: an aerial view of Ontario Place.

SUTTON

Suncor

Previous pages: the Toronto city skyline. Facing page: Ontario Place's rotund cinesphere emphasises the tall lines of yacht masts in the marina. Top: Nathan Phillips Square shading open-air artists. The Scarborough Civic Centre (above), in the biggest of the boroughs comprising Metropolitan Toronto, was opened in 1973. Its council chamber is housed underground. Overleaf: Toronto by night reflected in the waters of Lake Ontario.

Toronto Star

The borough of East York undertook restoration of Todmorden Mills (above and facing page top) in the city's Don area (these pages), as one of their centennial projects. Todmorden, the earliest industrial village of the Toronto area, supplied the growing nineteenth-century city with lumber, grain, whiskey, beer, paper and bricks. Its train station (facing page top), built in 1899, was relocated in 1969. Facing page bottom: the Central Don Stables, Sunnybrook Park, and (top and overleaf) Edward's Gardens.

DON

CENTRAL
DON
STABLES

Lake Ontario provides a scenic setting for Toronto (above), and affords such incongruous sights as a timeless-looking Norwegian clipper, the *Christian Radich* (facing page) under full sail, drawing towards a futuristic Toronto skyline; or the sleek, rigged American Coast Guard ship (top) cutting through the waters around Toronto. The lake is also the venue for one of the most important events of the Molson Winterfest, the ice canoe race (overleaf), providing a gruelling, six-kilometre course over Toronto's frozen harbour.

ALGARY

Casa Loma (facing page), described as "a mixture of seventeenth century Scottish baronial and Twentieth Century Fox", was built between 1911 and 1914 by the stockbroker Sir Henry Pellatt with money made partly from exploiting Niagara Falls for hydro-electricity. Its upkeep defeated him in the 1920s, and the city of Toronto claimed it for unpaid taxes. Spadina House (this page), built in the 1860s by another businessman, James Austin, was given to the Toronto Historical Board in 1982. Overleaf: Toronto's skyline by night.

THE WESTIN

From July 26 to August 1 the West Indian Caribana Festival is held on Toronto Islands by the Caribbean community. Moonlight cruises and a carnival ball culminate in Saturday's grand parade of steel bands and elaborately-costumed people (these pages) singing and dancing their way to the ferry docks. Overleaf: Christmas season in Nathan Phillips Square, when its illuminated, frozen pond becomes a skating rink by day.

digital

Sheraton Centre
MONTREAL TRUST
MONTREAL TRUST
National Trust
Admiral

Toronto's skyline (facing page and top) is now dominated by huge, modern office blocks and the sleek CN Tower, the world's tallest free-standing structure, whereas once sailors navigated by the outline of the Royal York Hotel and the spire of Holy Trinity Church. Storm-swept Lakeshore Boulevard boardwalk area (above) is home to several sailing clubs. Overleaf: Casa Loma, Sir Henry Pellatt's ninety-eight-room, castellated mansion.

Casa Loma

Ontario Place (this page), a huge, waterfront leisure park, is dominated by the global cinesphere with its six-storey-high, wraparound screen, capable of showing 70mm films. Toronto's mixture of open parks and highrise buildings (facing page) gives the largest city in Canada much of its appeal. Overleaf: the sound-proof, diamond-shaped panels of glass sheathing the Roy Thomson Hall are reflected, with an array of other lights, in the water.

HE WESTIN

Top: Dominion Day in Queen's Park, and (above) cheerfully-coloured houses in one of Toronto's attractive residential areas. Facing page: (top) Scarborough Bluffs, named by Governor Simcoe's wife for the English Yorkshire original, and (bottom) Black Creek Pioneer Village, frozen in time and temperature. Overleaf: a walkway to Ontario Place over a yacht marina.

MOLSONS

MALTING

This page: Ontario Place, and (facing page) the Old City Hall seen from Nathan Phillips Square. This officially opened its doors on September 18, 1899, to be superseded in 1965 by Viljo Revell's New City Hall. It has been preserved from developers by overwhelming popular insistence. Overleaf: Toronto at twilight, and (following page) St. James Cathedral, completed in 1853 and now framed by modern street cafés and shops.